Good King Wenceslas and the Chancellor of Bohemia

A Christmas Play

Tony Horitz

SAMUELFRENCH-LONDON.CO.UK
SAMUELFRENCH.COM

FOR AMATEUR PRODUCTION ENQUIRIES

UNITED KINGDOM AND WORLD
EXCLUDING NORTH AMERICA
plays@SamuelFrench-London.co.uk
020 7255 4302/01

Each title is subject to availability from Samuel French,

depending upon country of performance.

GOOD KING WENCESLAS AND THE CHANCELLOR OF BOHEMIA

The original production was devised by Tony Horitz, Graham Rogers, Sharon Sims, Mike Wardley and Pippa Weekes. The first performances were given at Scaplen's Court Museum, Poole, by Dorset Theatre in Education Team and Poole Museum's Advisory Teachers.

CHARACTERS

The Narrator, any age: male or female; may also play the **Storyteller** in Act I Scene 1
King Wenceslas, young: male
The Chancellor, middle-aged: male
The Page, younger than the King: male
First Servant, any age: male or female
Second Servant, any age: male or female
Third Servant, any age: male or female
Anna, the Innkeeper, middle-aged: female
Two Merchants, any age: male or female
Jacob, Anna's friend, any age: male
The Poor Man, middle-aged: male
Sara, the Poor Man's **Daughter**, young: female

Court Dancers, Neighbours, Travelling Players* etc.

NB Doubling. If desired, the Narrator can double as the Poor Man. The Three Servants can double as the Court Dancers in Act I, and as Anna and the Merchants, the Daughter and her Neighbours in Act II.

* A troupe of Travelling Players may be included if desired to mime the story told by the Narrator/Storyteller to the King during Act I Scene 1. The troupe could number anything between three and ten.

SYNOPSIS OF SCENES

ACT I

<table>
<tr><td>Scene 1</td><td>Introduction</td></tr>
<tr><td>Scene 2</td><td>At the Feast of St Stephen in the King's Banqueting Hall</td></tr>
<tr><td>Scene 3</td><td>In the Palace Courtyard</td></tr>
<tr><td>Scene 4</td><td>In the King's Private Chamber</td></tr>
</table>

ACT II

<table>
<tr><td>Scene 1</td><td>In the City Streets near the Chancellor's Mansion</td></tr>
<tr><td>Scene 2</td><td>In an Inn to the South of the City</td></tr>
<tr><td>Scene 3</td><td>By St Agnes' Fountain</td></tr>
<tr><td>Scene 4</td><td>In the Poor Man's Cottage close to the Fountain</td></tr>
</table>

PRODUCTION NOTES

1. The choice of incidental music for this play is left to the director's discretion. The songs are set to well-known traditional tunes for which no score is provided.

2. If desired, the audience can be encouraged to join in the dance in Act I, Scene 1, but this works best if a practice session is run as a 'Warm-Up' before the performance.

3. Several King Wenceslas myths have been combined in this play; this accounts for any historical inaccuracies or anachronisms to be found in the text.

ACT I

SCENE 1

Introduction

At the front of the stage is a raised dais on which a variety of props, relating to each of the characters in the play, is set out: a gold chain of office, a crown, a log, a joint of meat, a jug of wine, a Page's cap and a set of juggling balls. A psaltery, to be played by the Narrator, stands to one side

The CURTAIN *rises. The Company is standing behind the dais. They sing the traditional Victorian carol*

Song: Good King Wenceslas

All (*singing*) Good King Wenceslas looked out
On the Feast of Stephen,
When the snow lay round about,
Deep and crisp and even:
Brightly shone the moon that night,
Though the frost was cruel,
When a poor man came in sight
Gathering winter fuel.

'Hither, page, and stand by me,
If thou knowst it telling,
Yonder peasant, who is he?
Where and what his dwelling?'
'Sire, he lives a good league hence,
Underneath the mountain,
Right against the forest fence,
By St Agnes' fountain.'

'Bring me flesh, and bring me wine,
Bring me pine-logs hither:
Thou and I will see him dine,
When we bear them thither.'
Page and monarch, forth they went,
Forth they went together;
Through the rude wind's wild lament
And the bitter weather.

'Sire, the night is darker now,
And the wind blows stronger;
Fails my heart, I know not how;
I can go no longer.'
'Mark my footsteps, good my page;
Tread thou in them boldly:
Thou shalt find the winter's rage
Freeze thy blood less coldly.'

In his master's steps he trod,
Where the snow lay dinted;
Heat was in the very sod
Which the Saint had printed.
Therefore, Christian men, be sure,
Wealth or rank possessing,
Ye who now will bless the poor,
Shall yourselves find blessing.

The Narrator steps forward and plays a few chords on the psaltery before speaking

Narrator   Long long ago,
                        In Old Bohemia,
                        In the middle of Europe,
                        In the middle of winter,

                        Frost, ice and snow
                        Ruled the fields,
                        Raised their banner over all.

But in the halls
Of the great palaces
Friendly fires blazed
Through the short days
Through the long nights.

Long, long ago,
In old Bohemia,
In the middle of Europe,
In the middle of winter.

The Narrator plays a few more chords of music. During the following the actors playing the characters in the story step forward in turn to introduce themselves, each picking up the object from the dais that symbolizes his or her character before speaking. First, the Chancellor steps forward and picks up his golden chain of office

Chancellor   On the night of the Feast of Stephen,
The Chancellor gave a banquet,
A banquet fit for a King:
Many pigs were slain and roasted,
Many fish were hooked and grilled,
Many geese were plucked and boiled,
Many jugs of wine were filled.
No expense was spared
When the Chancellor gave a banquet.

The Narrator plays more music

The Chancellor exits

The actor playing the King now steps forward and picks up his crown as he speaks

The music stops

King   For the Chancellor's banquet
The young King was dressed
In his finest robes,

Made of softest velvet;
In his finest crown,
Trimmed with softest fur:
The King was dressed up
For the Chancellor's banquet.

The Narrator plays more music

The King exits

*The three Servants come and pick up a log for the fire, a large joint of meat
on a platter and a jug of wine*

The music stops

Servants (*together*) For the Chancellor's banquet,
                         Fit for the King,
                         The servants worked hard;
First Servant   Fetching wood ——
Second Servant — and food ——
Third Servant — and wine ——
All Servants   — for the Chancellor's banquet.

The Narrator plays more music

The Servants exit

The Page steps forward to pick up his cap and juggling balls

The music stops

Page   At the Chancellor's banquet,
                         Fit for the King,
                         The Chancellor's Page
                         Felt shy and nervous:
                         Seeing so much splendour,
                         Seeing so much luxury,
                         Seeing such a grand King
                         At the Chancellor's banquet.

The Narrator plays more music

The Page exits

The music stops

Narrator   Come, come with me
                      To the Chancellor's banquet,
                      Come, come and see
                      That feast fit for a King.

                      I'll be the Storyteller
                      At the Chancellor's banquet,
                      Listen and you'll hear
                      What happened there.

                      One night long ago,
                      In Old Bohemia,
                      In the middle of Europe,
                      In the middle of winter.

                      Come!

SCENE 2

At the Feast of St Stephen in the King's Banqueting Hall

The hall is decorated with regal banners and crests and a log fire burns in the fireplace. At one end of the hall is the King's table, laden with several kinds of food: meats, poultry, fish and cakes in abundance. King Wenceslas is sitting on a large chair behind the table with a goblet in his hand. He looks thoughtful. The Chancellor stands over him, also holding a goblet. He is smiling. Close by stands the Third Servant, holding a jug of wine, while the First Servant is holding a log basket by the fire . The Second Servant stands to one side of the table, with a tray of food. Also present are the King's Page and the Storyteller, who may be played by the Narrator

All the characters stand in a freeze until the Narrator brings them to life with music

Chancellor A little more to eat, Your Majesty? (*To the Second Servant*) Come, bring the sweet. Hurry up!

The Second Servant hurries forward with the tray

King I have had enough, thank you, Chancellor.
Chancellor Come now, Sire, you must eat — to keep up your strength. A King must feast well to make himself strong and healthy. A sliver of boar's head, perhaps?
King (*a little impatiently*) I've told you already, Chancellor, I'm full up. I don't want any more.
Chancellor If you insist, Sire, but I do hope you will not grow ill. (*To the Second Servant*) Servant! Take that food back to the kitchen. Then clear the table. (*To the Third Servant*) Bring more wine for His Majesty. Well, what are you waiting for?

The Servant serves wine to the King and the Chancellor, then goes to refill the wine jug

(*Raising his goblet to propose a toast*) Your Majesty, King Wenceslas, Great and Good Ruler of all Bohemia, I toast your health on this, the feast of St Stephen! (*To the First Servant*) Put more wood on the fire! We don't want the King to catch cold, do we? Dear me, no!

The First Servant obeys. The three Servants clear the table and fetch more wine during the following dialogue. Meanwhile the King and the Chancellor whisper together

First Servant Just look at all this food the King's left.
Second Servant What'll happen to it?
First Servant It'll be thrown to the pigs — to fatten them up.

The Chancellor walks towards the Servants during the following and stops close to them, making them aware of his presence

Third Servant (*joining in*) What a waste! He's hardly touched a thing.
Second Servant And when you think how hungry most ——

Chancellor I thought I told you to clear the table?

The Servants silently hurry to obey the Chancellor. They continue to do so until the Chancellor gives them their next command. Meanwhile the Page starts practising juggling

And now, Your Majesty, I have arranged for your pleasure some entertainment of the highest order.

King Oh good, Chancellor. Is your young Page going to juggle for me? I have noticed him practising.

The Page steps forwards eagerly and starts to juggle

Chancellor (*pushing the Page back to his original position*) No, Sire, my page does not juggle yet. He needs more practice. Much more practice. No, Sire. I have engaged, at considerable expense, the finest dancers in the kingdom of Bohemia. Tonight, in your great court, they will perform just for you.

King (*looking pleased*) Excellent.

The Chancellor claps his hands

The dancers appear, performing a slow courtly dance to music

King I enjoyed that. Well done, everyone. (*He applauds*)

Chancellor Thank you, Sire. Most gracious. But now I offer you something even better — a wonderful jester who is said to be the finest Storyteller in the land. May his words please Your Majesty and give you good digestion. (*He smiles at the King. He then turns to the Narrator, his face taking on a threatening look, and summons him with a gesture*)

The Narrator moves forward to join the Chancellor

(*Whispering threateningly to the Narrator*) This story had better be good! (*He moves away, smiling again at the King*) Sire, the Storyteller!

The Narrator looks about him and bows to the King. The story he tells can be related in traditional form or 'enacted' by a mime troupe as the words are spoken

Narrator Your Majesty, I bring you a story I learnt in a far-off land. It tells of a King so grand, he would be as a peacock to your butterfly. This King, who lived long ago, had a palace similar to your own, with great tall ceilings and the finest of decorations. And in this King's palace there was so much gold that it had to be stacked right up to those great tall ceilings. Every day more gold was carried to the palace from every corner of the world. They say this gold shone like the sun itself, glittering both day and night. But in spite of owning so much wealth the King was restless; bored. He wanted something else, something that no other King possessed. So he summoned his loyal and trusted Adviser, a man of great stature and self-importance, rather like your own Chancellor, Sire. Well this Adviser was a very clever man. He had two brilliant ideas. The first was to build a special carriage, with a great catapult attached to the front and a wide net attached to the back. This contraption would be pulled by six white horses through the streets before the King's Procession and clear away all the poor people and all the rubbish spoiling his view.

Chancellor (*interrupting*) Oh really! His Majesty does not want to hear stupid stories about miserable poor people on a happy occasion such as this — the Feast of St Stephen. Do you, Sire?

King Let the Storyteller continue, Chancellor.

Chancellor As Your Majesty wishes.

King (*to the Narrator*) What was the second brilliant idea?

Narrator Ah! To build a tower! Now, the King in my story was very pleased when he heard of the plan to clear the streets of rubbish. But he was even more excited when the Adviser told him of the golden tower to the stars. Yes, the Adviser described how some of the King's glittering gold would be carried out of the palace and used as bricks to build the tallest tower in the world — so tall indeed that the King could climb to the very top and touch the stars themselves. Everyone thought this a marvellous idea. Everyone in the court cheered and clapped. Everyone that it is except Zito, the King's jester. Zito was so small he was almost invisible and he used to hide in the most unusual places. (*From underneath his cloak he produces a puppet jester which he uses rather like a ventriloquist's dummy. The Narrator moves close to the King with the puppet, as if to speak to him*) 'Sire,' said Zito, 'I have another idea, a better one in my humble opinion. If you really wish for that which you do not own, then you must go to the dark damp swamp in the south of the city. There if you go carefully you may find an island

and on that island by a simple weeping willow tree you will find that which you do not own — indeed, that which you cannot own.' Well when the King heard Zito's suggestion he was not pleased. 'What kind of stupid riddle is this?' he roared. 'Get out of my sight.' Everyone in the court jeered at Zito. 'How dare you insult His Majesty!' exclaimed the Adviser. 'Allow me to deal with the rapscalion, Sire.' And before Zito could utter another word he was taken out of the palace and thrown head first into the swamp at the south of the city, never to enter the palace gates again. (*He hurls the puppet across the floor*). The King soon forgot about him, with all the excitement over the tower. Everyone in the city was set to work moving gold to the site, then carefully laying the gold bricks down on top of each other. Day by day the tower grew taller and taller until it reached up like a pointing finger — right above the palace itself and up into the clouds. The King was thrilled. The day came for him to open it. He entered through a golden arched door at the very bottom and climbed the winding golden staircase that had been especially built inside. Up, up he went, higher and higher. At the very top he opened a door onto a golden balcony and felt giddy with emotion. There just above him was a sparkling star, the jewelled belt of Orion. It would be his! He stretched out his arm towards it and — it was just out of reach. Then he saw another star that was just a little closer — the Evening Star, Venus itself. Yes, this was the one! The King reached out again — it was almost in his grasp — surely — again he stretched — and stretched — but as he stretched the tower began to wobble — it was so top-heavy with gold it could not support his weight. It wobbled again — and the King grew giddier and giddier — until he fell from the tower. Down, down he fell, like a wounded bird ——

Chancellor (*interrupting again more forcefully. He moves over to remove the Narrator as he speaks*) That's it. That is quite enough! How dare you tell stories of Kings falling from towers, do you want to give His Majesty nightmares? Come on, away with you ——

King Stop! Chancellor, please let the Storyteller finish. He was just getting to the most exciting part of the story. Try not to interrupt any more. (*To the Narrator*) Please continue. Was the King killed by the fall?(*He remains spell-bound by the story until the end*)

Narrator No, Sire, for his royal cloak spread like a pair of wings and carried him away on the wind to another part of the city, which he had never visited. There he floated down and landed in a tree. But it was a dark and dangerous part of the city — full of thieves. And as two of these thieves saw the King land they quickly came and stripped him of his fine clothes while he hung helpless in the tree. They left him their dirty rags and ran off laughing. Well, the poor King finally untangled himself and was forced to put on the rags left by the thieves. Then he tried to return to the palace. But he was lost. Whenever he saw people he asked them the way, saying that he was the King. But they just laughed at him and threw mud and stones at him, taking him for a fool. The King had to hide in a dark and dingy alley. Cold and tired he fell asleep, with only rubbish and rats for companions. Then, in the middle of the night, a strange and terrible noise awoke him. It was the sound of huge hoofs clattering on city cobblestones, coming nearer and nearer. Suddenly the noise stopped, only to be followed by an even worse grinding sound as a long monstrous neck with claws instead of a head reached towards the King. Helpless, he was plucked into the air and tossed into a huge net. What monster was it? Shaking with fear the King remembered the Adviser's first suggestion — the Rubbish Clearing Carriage! The King was taken to the south of the city along with many other poor people who were collected by the Rubbish Clearing Carriage on the way. Early the next morning a large, braying crowd assembled to watch. There at the front of them stood the King's Adviser — wearing the King's own crown on his head. He began bellowing out orders to the Carriage's Operator. Wearing a hooded mask, this man pulled a lever which released the catapult at the back of the Carriage. One by one the poor people caught in the net were hurtled through the air only to land in the swamp beyond. Thwack! went the Operator. Thwack! And thwack again! Finally it came to the King's turn. 'Stop, I beg you!' he cried. 'I am your King, your true King.' But the crowd just laughed and threw rotten vegetables and mud at him. 'The King was killed when he fell from the tower,' shouted the Adviser. 'Throw this wretched liar into the swamp!' Thwack! went the Operator and the King was sent flying into the air. He landed with a splash in the middle of the disgusting, smelly swamp. He began to sink deeper and deeper into the mud. It oozed into his nose, his mouth and his eyes. He struggled and struggled and just managed to catch hold of an overhanging branch. Then he hauled himself along through the mud until he reached the island in the middle of the swamp. The King clambered to safety underneath a weeping willow tree and crawled over the dust. Suddenly, he noticed something tiny in front of him. It was a skeleton, the skeleton of his jester Zito. And Zito's finger was pointing to some words scratched in the dust. The King stared at them and he could just make out the three words, 'I forgive you'. And that, Sire, is my story, the story of the King who had everything but wanted more and so ended with nothing.

There is a long silence. Then the King claps, followed by the Chancellor. The Narrator makes to leave but is stopped by the King

King Storyteller, a word. I think the King in your tale would have been wiser to have listened to his fool Zito rather than his Adviser. Am I right?
Narrator Sire, the task of the Storyteller is to lead the listener into the woods, not to say which is the right path through.

The Narrator exits

The King looks thoughtful

Chancellor What a good thing it is, King Wenceslas, that in your kingdom there are no wretched, poor people like those described in that rather miserable story. For in Bohemia everyone has plenty to eat and drink. Everyone is warm and happy.
King (*uncertainly*) Yes.
Chancellor And what a good thing, too, we in Bohemia have such a fine and generous King. So different from the one in the story. But Sire you look sad. Tut-Tut! It is the Feast of St Stephen. You should be happy. Well, I have a little present planned for you, which will I hope put a smile on your royal visage. Sire, I take great pleasure in announcing that I, your loyal Chancellor, am going to have something very, very special built for you.
King A tower, perhaps?
Chancellor Oh no, Sire. Far too dangerous. No, King Wenceslas of Bohemia is to have a new statue. I myself have personally overseen the plans, designed by the finest, most accomplished architects in Bohemia.
King May I see them, Chancellor?
Chancellor No need, Your Majesty. For I have arranged something even better. I have arranged for a model of the statue to be erected outside in the courtyard , on the very spot where the real statue will finally be placed. Now if Your Majesty will just spare me a few moments I will go and ensure everything is ready. Then perhaps you would care to step graciously out onto your balcony to view the model? (*He clicks his fingers to the Servants*)

The Servants hurry off, followed by the Chancellor

*The Narrator enters, plays a few chords on the psaltery, then steps
forward to address the audience*

Narrator   The young King sat
                      As still as a statue
                      The young King waited
                      To look at the statue.
                      And while he waited
                      The young King thought
                      About the other King
                      In the story he had heard.

Music

SCENE 3

In the Palace Courtyard

*A balcony overlooks the acting area. Royal banners hang around the
stage. The only specific property necessary for this scene is a pile of logs
for firewood. The Narrator gestures appropriately to the acting area*

Narrator   As for the Chancellor, he was busy.
                      Outside in the cobbled courtyard

*The Chancellor and the three Servants enter. The Chancellor is carry-
ing a lance. During the following, the Chancellor moulds the Servants
into position to become the statue of the King on horseback, one
kneeling down to make the back end of the horse, another kneeling up
to make the front of the horse, the third sitting astride the first,
representing the King himself. The Chancellor puts the lance into this
Servant's hand*

                      With the soft snow swept clean
                      Three servants were needed
                      To model the statue of the King.

> Outside in the cobbled courtyard
> With the soft snow swept clean
> A poor man suddenly appeared
> Searching for firewood there.

The Poor Man appears, unseen at first by the Chancellor. He waits for a chance to take some of the logs

Chancellor (*giving instructions and adjusting the statue*) Hmm — Weapon up a bit — yes — Horse — ears —

The Servants obey at once, the Servant forming the front of the horse using hands to represent the horse's ears. Meanwhile, the Poor Man sneaks out and picks up a log

Yes, that's just about — (*He stops, as he catches sight of the Poor Man*) Hey! What are you doing?

Poor Man (*nervously*) I'm ... just ... collecting a bit of wood, sir, for the fire, sir.

Chancellor (*snatching the log away*) Oh no you don't! You do not collect firewood here, you stupid peasant. Poor person, you! Clear off out of here! And don't you dare come within one hundred leagues of the Royal Palace again.

The Poor Man beats a hasty retreat, running off

(*Aiming a kick at the Poor Man*) Honestly! (*He turns on the Servants*)

The Servants quake with fear, causing the Servant forming the front of the horse to wring his hands and forget about the ears

Did you let him in?

The Servants shake their heads

I've told you before. No poor people are allowed anywhere near the Palace. Ever! (*He hurls the log down*)

The Servants jump

(To the Servant forming the horse's ears; shouting) EARS!

The Servant immediately makes the horse's ears again

Will somebody kindly tell the King that his statue is ready to be looked at? Page! *(He gets increasingly more irate as the speech progresses)* Just how long do I have to stand here in the cold? Really! Here I am with a special statue ready for the King and he can't even be bothered to come out here and look at it!

The Page appears on the balcony, followed closely by the King

King Is something the matter, Chancellor?
Chancellor Oh no, Your Majesty. Nothing at all. *(He gestures to the statue)* The statue, Sire. Of course, this is only a model, a pale shadow of the finished article, which will be covered in gold as befits your gracious ——
King *(interrupting)* Don't I look rather stern?
Chancellor *(to the Servant sitting on the horse)* Smile!

The Servant obeys immediately

You see, Sire. Anything can be changed.
King What am I sitting on?
Chancellor A horse, Sire. You are here — *(he points to the Servant on top)* — the horse is underneath. *(He points to the other Servants)*
King *(thoughtfully)* It's a long time since I rode a horse.
Chancellor Too dangerous, Sire. We mustn't risk any nasty accidents.
King *(impatiently)* Yes, that's what you always say. But I hate staying shut up in this palace.
Chancellor You owe it to your people to keep safe, Your Majesty. You are still young, you have a long life ahead of you. Plenty of time for adventures.
King I'm not a child, Chancellor. Anyway, if I'm allowed a say in this statue, then I'd like the horse to be galloping ... through open fields.
Chancellor Certainly, Sire. *(He smacks the Servant forming the front of the horse)*

The Servant rears upwards. The Servant forming the rear of the horse puts his arms through those of the front Servant to suggest other legs galloping

The Poor Man sneaks on and tries again to steal firewood

The Chancellor sees the Poor Man and emits an involuntary groan. The King spots him too

King Who is that man?

The Chancellor pushes the Poor Man towards the exit

Chancellor (*quietly*) I thought I told you to clear off?

The Chancellor pushes the Poor Man off

(*To the King*) Nothing to worry yourself about, Sire.
King But who is he? He looks poor.
Chancellor (*ignoring him*) He's nobody, Sire. (*Changing the subject*) Dear me, hasn't it turned cold suddenly? You had better go back indoors to your Royal Chambers. Remember what the royal doctors said, Sire. You must look after your health. You owe it to your people.
King I want an explanation, Chancellor.
Chancellor And you shall have one, Sire. Later. Soon. I shall come to your chambers. I promise.
King Good.

The King steps back inside the palace followed by the Page

The Chancellor bows low for a very long time. Suddenly he straightens up and turns on the Servants

Well, don't just stand there like dummies. Pack it all up. *(Aside)* If I get my hands on that wood thief...

The Chancellor exits. The Servants head in the opposite direction, whispering as they go

First Servant It's not fair, it really isn't!
Second Servant Hold your tongue — if you want to keep it!
Third Servant If only someone could do something!

They exit

Music

Scene 4

In the King's Private Chamber

A fire is blazing in the hearth. A large chest is set on one side of the fire with a jug of wine on it. The King stands on the other side, holding a goblet of wine and looking thoughtful

Narrator   When the King saw the Poor Man
The Chancellor was cross.
For a few icy seconds
He seemed to be lost.
The King had seen a poor man
Where none were meant to be.
For a few icy seconds
The truth had wriggled free.

But the King must not know
What is happening in his nation
So the Chancellor must prepare
A proper explanation.
See how the King is standing
Close by a roaring fire;
Questions have flared up in his head
Can his Chancellor be a liar?

King   (*thinking aloud*)   I wonder who that man in rags was? The Chancellor keeps telling me there are no poor people in my kingdom — so why was that man here? I am not sure if I trust the Chancellor any more.

The door opens and the Chancellor enters with the Page. They stand some distance from the King, in the shadows. The Chancellor holds the Page close and speaks quietly but severely to him

Chancellor   Next time I ask you to fetch the King, you do it quickly. Understand? Now stand over there!

The Page obeys, moving to the other side of the room

(*Smiling and bowing to the King*) And how did you like your statue, Your Majesty?

King It will be perfect, I am sure, Chancellor. But, tell me, what will it be made of?

Chancellor Of the finest gold, Sire. As I promised. Gold from head to toe.

King Won't that cost a great deal of money? Who will pay?

Chancellor (*approaching the King*) I would like you to consider the statue a present. A little gift from me to you, on this the Feast of St Stephen.

King (*not quite convinced*) Ah! I understand. Thank you. (*He pauses*) Who was that stranger in the courtyard?

The Chancellor looks blank

I mean the man looking for firewood.

Chancellor Your Majesty, I am so sorry you had to witness that terrible scene. The man was nothing but a common thief who had forced his way into the courtyard.

King But he looked so weak — so poor — so hungry.

Chancellor Sire, I fear your young eyes have been blinded by the snow. All people in your kingdom have enough food to eat, wine to drink and firewood to keep them warm through this long, cruel winter. The only trouble is, one or two are greedy. Even though they have more than enough, they still go around stealing things to sell in the market-place.

King But where does that man come from?

Chancellor Who knows, Sire? From a village in the south of the city, I believe. You wouldn't know the place, Sire.

King No, I probably wouldn't. Seeing as I never leave the palace.

Chancellor Oh, dear. Your Majesty must realize I have only your own good at heart.

King Perhaps so. But as this winter has been especially bad, maybe I should visit the countryside of Bohemia and just make sure everyone is well and happy.

Chancellor Oh no, Sire. That would never do. No, no, no. It's far too cold for you to travel. Not at this time of the year. The doctors would never allow it. And besides, think of all the duties you have to perform here. Things to open, things to talk about, things to look at, things to shut.

King (*angry*) I feel like a prisoner in my own palace. A King should be able to go where he pleases.

Chancellor (*coming very close to the King and seizing his hand; lovingly*) Now please don't start getting yourself upset, Sire. Just think of the terrible weather out there. You have a responsibility to your subjects to keep fit and well. Snow, blizzards, ice and gales. It's just not the right time of year to travel anywhere.

King But I want to visit my kingdom!

Chancellor And so you shall, Sire. So you shall. In the spring, when the fine weather comes. Then like the fresh green leaves on the trees, so King Wenceslas shall appear in Bohemia.

King (*realizing he cannot win*) Very well, Chancellor.

Chancellor It is for your own good, Your Majesty,

King Yes, I am sure. (*He pauses*) You may go, Chancellor.

Chancellor Thank you, Sire. I do have a small party of my own to attend to at home. (*He crosses to the Page and whispers to him*) You are to stay here tonight and keep an eye on the King. He must not leave the palace. On no account. Understand?

Page Yes, Chancellor.

Chancellor (*crossing to the door and bowing to the King*) Good-night, Your Royal Majesty. I will leave you my Page to keep you company on this, the night of the Blessed St Stephen.

The King makes no reply, turning instead to face the fire

The Chancellor exits

There is a pause. Eventually the King speaks, with his back to the Page

King How old are you, Page?

Page Fourteen, Sire.

King How long have you served the Chancellor?

Page Six months, Sire.

King Is he a good master?

Page (*after a slight pause*) Oh yes, Sire. I am very fortunate to be in the service of such a great man.

King Yes. And where did you live before you became the Chancellor's Page?

Page In a small village to the South of the city, Sire. Near St Agnes' fountain.

King Ah yes. The Holy Fountain of St Agnes. She was an ancestor of mine. Did you know that?

Page Yes, Your Majesty.

King My grandfather's sister. And yet I have never visited her fountain, where she found holy water. (*He pauses*) Bring me more wine.

The Page obeys immediately, moving to the chest to pick up the jug and fill the King's goblet. As he starts to withdraw the King stops him

Wait! That man in the courtyard — he was from the South wasn't he?

Page What man, Sire?

King The one taking the wood.

Page Yes, Sire. He lives in a village close to mine, right at the edge of the forest.

King So you know him, then?

Page Yes, Sire.

King Is he a thief?

Page Oh no, Sire.

King Your master, the Chancellor says he is. Is he lying?

Page Certainly not, Sire. He must be mistaken, confusing the man with — you see, there are so many —— (*He stops himself quickly, realizing he has said too much*)

King So many what, Page? Thieves? Poor people?

The Page hangs his head

I knew it! I knew it! But why did he come all the way to the palace looking for wood? Why doesn't he just take it from the trees where he lives?

Page Because they all belong to you, Sire. It is a crime to take wood from the King's forests. Only old, dead wood may be taken — and that is all covered with snow.

King I see. Right, that's it! (*He moves about, thinking quickly*) So you know where this poor man lives?

Page Yes, his cottage is right under the mountain.

King Good. So you'll be able to show me the way there.

Page (*worried*) Sire? What do you mean?

King (*standing close and speaking in lowered tones*) You're coming with me on a journey.

Page When, Sire?

King Tonight. On this, the Feast of St Stephen, we will take presents to that poor man.

Page But, Your Majesty — you mustn't — it's too cold out ——

King Not you, too! I am going to St Agnes' fountain now, tonight. You will lead the way.

Page I cannot, Sire.
King Why not?
Page The Chancellor, Sire; he made me promise to keep you here.
King Obey me now and I promise to make sure everything is all right for
you and your family. Trust me!

The Page is unconvinced

I am your King! Now, there's no time to waste. Go to the kitchens, fetch
the finest meat you can find — a large joint of beef or ham and a flagon
of strong red wine — oh, and some pine logs! Put them in a basket and
meet me in the courtyard in a minute.Well, don't just stand there, go!
Page (*aside*) It's all right for him — I'm the one who'll be in trouble ...
King (*calling after him*) And, Page! Don't tell anyone about this. It's our
secret.

The Page exits

*The King opens the chest and rummages round. Finally he takes out a
large hood*

I'll go in disguise, so no-one will recognize me, like the King in the
Jester's story... (*He takes off his crown and puts it in the chest*) The King
shall stay in the palace; Wenceslas shall go into Bohemia. We shall see
if all is as well as the Chancellor claims.

The King exits hurriedly

Narrator   So Wenceslas left his palace
                      On that cold and snowy night
                      Taking gifts of winter solace
                      To refresh and to delight.

                      Only the Page went with him
                      On that cold and snowy night
                      Hunch-backed against the cold
                      They made an unusual sight.

                      What truths would the King learn

On that cold and snowy night?
Was he sinking into the darkness
Or heading up into the light?

CURTAIN

ACT II

SCENE 1

In the City Streets near the Chancellor's Mansion

Various tall buildings covered with snow. The front doorway of the Chancellor's Mansion is to one side

The Page enters from the side of the stage opposite the Chancellor's house, carrying a large basket full of meat, wine and logs. The King enters behind the Page, hooded, carrying a lantern

Narrator
Through freshly-fallen snow,
King and Page go
On the coldest night of the year,
With hoods pulled down
They move through the town,
The warm palace left behind.
Will their journey together
In the bitter weather
Bring happiness or despair?

The young King's eyes
Are filled with surprise
At everything he sees,
But the young Page's eyes
Cannot disguise
The fear that freezes within.

The Page stops suddenly, looking worried

King (*excited*) It's amazing! All this snow! It's so bright, so white! Listen how it scrunches under my feet!
Page Sssh! Sire!

King What is it? Why have you stopped?
Page (*after a pause*) He may hear us, Sire.
King Who may hear us?
Page The Chancellor. His house is just over the street. (*He points to the Chancellor's house close by*)
King But he won't recognize me. You needn't worry.
Page What if he recognizes me, Sire?
King We'll think of something. Come on, or else we'll never reach the poor man's cottage tonight. I'll lead the way. (*He raises the lantern*) Follow me. Everything will be all right.

The King and the Page, the latter carrying the basket, move across the acting area, passing the door of the Chancellor's house. Just as they are almost safely past, the door flies open

The Chancellor appears. He grabs the Page by the scruff of the neck. The King stands back, in the shadows

Chancellor Just where do you think you're going?
Page (*nervously, gesturing to the basket*) I'm just taking the scraps to the pigs, Chancellor.
Chancellor Who ordered you to do that?
Page Er ... The Royal Head Cook, Chancellor. I'm to return immediately.
Chancellor The Royal Head Cook's off duty tonight.
Page He left a message for me — before he went home.
Chancellor (*suspicious*) Hmm. Let's have a look in that basket.

The King coughs

(*To the King*) Who are you?
King I am a pilgrim. I am travelling to the holy shrine of St Agnes. This young man met me on the way and has offered to point me in the right direction.
Chancellor St Agnes' Fountain, eh? Have you paid your Pilgrim's Tax?
King What tax would that be, Sir?
Chancellor All travellers in Bohemia must pay pilgrimage taxes to me.
King And who are you, Sir?
Chancellor Mind your own business. (*Holding out his hand*) Five crowns! Pay up.

The King gives the Chancellor five crowns, keeping his head down

On your way!

Both the King and the Page move to exit

Chancellor (*stopping the Page*) Just a minute! You! Remember —as soon as you've thrown the scraps to the pigs go straight back to the palace and check the King. Hurry it up!

The King and the Page leave quickly

Pilgrimage to St Agnes's Fountain, eh? There's something strange going on here. I'll follow them. (*Calling into the house*) Servants! Fetch my winter coat!

The Chancellor exits into his house

Music

SCENE 2

In an Inn to the South of the City

A simple inn, with sparse furnishings. A rocking chair is set by an open fire. Near it are two benches and a table, with a jug and some tankards on it. Over the fire is a mantelpiece, with some meagre Christmas decorations on it, including a stick of holly, a sprig of pine, some red ribbon and a sugar mouse. Sitting on the rocking chair, the innkeeper, Anna, is telling a story— the same one we heard in the Banquet Scene in Act One. We do not hear her at first, just see her gestures as she mimes telling the tale. Near her are Jacob, a regular, and two Travelling Merchants, sitting on one of the benches. They each hold a tankard from which they drink from time to time and there are bags of merchandise at their feet

Narrator   In an Inn beside the city walls
                      Travellers shelter from the cold
                      Warming themselves by the fire
                      Listening to tales of old

> Tonight the Innkeeper may receive
> Two more travelling men
> But if they enter in disguise
> Will she recognize them?

Anna's voice becomes audible now

Anna And so the King fell in the swamp, he did, and he grabbed hold of this old branch and he did pull and pull with all his might, until he reached the bank. And then he looked up and what did he see ? Well, he did see a shiny skeleton, big as a giant, white as the snow outside this window. And the finger of this huge, gleaming skeleton, it was pointing towards the King himself. And in the dirty mud what do you think was written?

Others We don't know! Tell us, Anna!

Anna In the dirty mud it was written: 'I forgive you'.

All react to the story at once, nodding their heads and muttering with appreciation

Jacob A good story, Anna, a fine one. I seem to have heard it before somewhere. (*To Merchants*) Have you ever heard it?

Merchants (*exchanging glances*) No.

Anna Where did you say you were from?

First Merchant From Persia.

Jacob Where's that then?

Second Merchant Persia is long way from here.

First Merchant Long, long way. To South.

Second Merchant Where sun shines.

First Merchant Not like here. Not cold.

Second Merchant Too cold here. Much too cold.

The Merchants shiver

Anna (*pointing to the tankards the Merchants are holding*) Well, you drink up our fine ale and you'll soon warm yourselves.

A knock on the door is heard

More visitors!

Jacob Your luck's in tonight, Anna.

Anna Well, hurry up and open the door, Jacob, or they'll go away and we'll lose their custom.

Jacob You never know — it may be King Wenceslas!

Anna (*laughing*) Ha! That'll be the day! Hey — more likely the Chancellor! (*She spits*)

Jacob opens the door

King Wenceslas, still in disguise, enters accompanied by the Page with the basket. Neither Jacob nor Anna recognise either of them

Come in, strangers, and welcome. Come in and warm yourselves by my fire. Sit yourselves down. (*She motions the King and the Page to the bench*)

They sit

Jacob, fetch a mug of ale for these young gentlemen.

Jacob does so

What brings you to these parts, then?

King We are on a journey — a pilgrimage to St Agnes' Fountain.

Anna Really? It's many months since we had people rest here on a journey to that Holy place. You must be true Christians. On such a cold night as this.

Jacob You'd better hurry too. By the time you get there the Chancellor will have put a tax on the Holy Water! Isn't that so, Anna?

Anna (*laughing*) He's put tax on everything else! Still as long as I've customers in my inn, I'll make out, I suppose. (*She points to the Merchants*) These two merchants have travelled all the way from — where was it?

Merchants Persia. We are coming for the Bohemia Christmas fair. To sell our fine goods.

Jacob laughs loudly

Anna It's no laughing matter, Jacob.

First Merchant Why does he laugh?

Anna Because there is no Christmas fair this year.

Second Merchant What do you mean?

First Merchant We travel far, all this way for great Bohemia Christmas fair.

Anna It's sad but it's true. There won't be a proper Christmas at all this year. Do you know what I've got to give my children? (*She picks up the sugar mouse from the mantelpiece*) This sugar mouse! What with that, this little pine twig and this old ribbon that belonged to my grand-mother — it's not going to be much of a Christmas for my family.

Second Merchant But we are hearing there is much money in Bohemia.

First Merchant For this we have travelled so long a way.

Anna I am afraid you heard wrong.

Second Merchant But we have such fine goods to sell. (*He brings a puppet out of one of his bags*) Look at this beautiful puppet. Yes, beautiful for your children. Look, look how he walks, look how he moves, how he dances! (*He makes the puppet perform for them*) You must surely buy one of these beautiful puppets.

Anna I'd love to. How much?

Second Merchant Only five crowns.

Anna That's far too much. Five crowns would keep us in food for two days.

Second Merchant So, then — four gold crowns, only.

Anna We've no spare money.

The First Merchant springs into action, bringing out carpets and clothes. He shows a Persian rug to the King

First Merchant But just you look at this rug. Feel the quality, this is finest Persian rug, this is best.

Anna Oh, it is lovely.

First Merchant Only fifteen crowns, special price for you.

Anna But I've no money _ don't you understand?

First Merchant Only twelve, twelve crowns!

Jacob You're wasting your time.

The First Merchant takes a small brocade waistcoat to the King

First Merchant You, Sir. You like this? For the boy? Seven gold pieces!

The King hesitates, then fetches the money from a velvet purse. The Page tries to stop the King but is ignored

Thank you, kind gentleman. Here is your waistcoat. (*He hands the waistcoat to the King: to Anna*) You say there is no money! Ha!

Anna (*addressing the King*) You must be mad. I'd have given you a week's board and lodging for that much!

Jacob (*lying on the Persian rug*) And bought us all drinks!

First Merchant (*to Jacob, crossly*) You want Persian rug? Then you must pay — like him (*he gestures to the King*). Twelve golden crowns. Or get off!

Jacob (*reluctantly getting off the rug*) I was only trying it for size.

Anna I'm telling you, Persians — the only place you'll find money around here is up at the palace.

Jacob True enough. Didn't you see it as you entered the city?

Anna Yes, it's hard to miss it — what with the gleaming golden towers.

Jacob That's where the money all goes. In taxes to keep the King in gold.

Anna They have huge banquets up there, hundreds of people come.

Jacob Yes. They eat and drink until they're so stuffed they can't even get through the doors. So then they have to sleep together in a great big pile in the Main Hall. It's true! There's enough grub in that palace to feed the whole country, believe me!

Anna And the wine flows like the water from St Agnes' fountain.

Second Merchant So you're saying that all people have nothing, but King has everything?

Jacob Yes! Most people are starving.

Anna But, Jacob — do you know what's worse? Do you know what I've heard the dear Chancellor is having built for the King?

Jacob What?

Anna A statue, that's what. A statue of a galloping horse with oh, so fine a rider on top — the King himself!

Jacob Never! He doesn't know a horse from a wild boar!

Anna The King on horseback, I tell you — and what's more, all to be made of finest gold.

King (*almost forgetting his disguise*) But wait! I have heard that the Chancellor is to pay for this statue himself.

Anna and Jacob laugh loudly

Anna Where have you come from?

Jacob Best joke I've heard in a long while! The Chancellor paying indeed!

Anna We're paying! That's why we are so poor. We're taxed for everything. Inn Tax, Village Tax, House Tax, Merchants' Tax, Pilgrims' Tax — you name it!

Jacob (*pointing to the rug*) Carpet Tax!

Anna They'd tax the air we breathe if they could.

Second Merchant So this Chancellor, he takes tax money from you and spends it on the King.

Anna That's right.

Second Merchant This is terrible!

First Merchant It is clear we will make no money here. We must go back home.

Anna In this weather? Look outside, Jacob.

Jacob (*going to the window*) Snow as deep as an ocean.

First Merchant We too have little money. How can we stay here?

Anna You can't travel in this snow. I'll tell you what I'll do. That fine Persian rug of yours — you can stay here for a couple of nights and in return I'll have that rug for my floor. And I'll do you some food.

Jacob Food's better than last year. We got snowed in for two weeks then. No food left, so we ended up eating rats.

Anna Boiled rats, baked rats, roast rats, fried rats ...

Jacob Now the fried rats were quite tasty. (*To the King and the Page*) Ever tried fried rats?

First Merchant It seems we must stay.

Second Merchant Oh dear! What will become of us?

Anna Ah, well. I may be able to help you there.

Jacob She can tell the future, can Anna. (*To Anna*) Shall I fetch the sticks?

Anna Very well, Jacob.

Jacob (*fetching sticks from the fireplace*) She's good, you know.

Anna This is how we spend the long winter's nights in Bohemia. (*She kneels with the sticks in her hands and concentrates, closing her eyes*)

First Merchant What does she do now?

Jacob Sssh! Don't interrupt—else it won't work!

Second Merchant Very strange.

Anna moves the sticks in a dramatic circular motion through the air as she moans meaningfully. Finally she drops the sticks on the ground, where they fall in a pattern

Anna (*as she examines the first stick*) Now, travellers, let's see. Well, you're not going to do very well in Bohemia.
First Merchant This we are already knowing.
Jacob Sssh!
Anna (*looking at the next stick*) But when you return to your own country, your luck will change. You may even become famous.

The Merchants smile

Anna (*looking at the next stick*) Now this is interesting.
Second Merchant What?
Anna Three sticks in the shape of a triangle. (*She looks hard at the Merchants*). You are going to let someone in this room down badly. Maybe even betray them!
Merchants No! It is not true.
Anna The sticks never lie. Do they Jacob?
Jacob They never lie. Except on the ground!
Anna (*To the King*) What about you, pilgrim?

The King looks as if he is about to agree to have the sticks thrown for him but the Page stops him with a nod of his head

Suit yourself.
Jacob Do mine, do mine! See if I'm going to end up with a golden statue like the King.

Anna shakes the sticks as before; Jacob joins in with the moaning noises. Anna throws the sticks down

What do they say? Tell me!
Anna (*picking up the first stick*) Well, Jacob, you're going to fall on hard times.

Jacob looks disappointed

(*Picking up the next stick*) Then, you're going to fall on worse times.

Jacob looks more disappointed

(*Picking up the next stick*) Then you're going to have absolutely nothing. You'll lose everything.

Jacob looks devastated

(*Picking up the next stick*) But wait! This looks promising. You are going to gain something after all.

Jacob (*excitedly*) What? What?

Anna Warts. See, look at all those knobbly bits on the stick!

Jacob is even more downcast

Not to worry, because you're going to live to a fine old age, even though you probably won't have any friends, nor a roof over your head. Still, better luck next time, eh, Jacob?

Jacob (*shrugging his shoulders in resignation*) Come on, Anna, give me the sticks. I'll throw them for you. (*He takes the sticks and overdoes the actions*) Like this?

Anna Not so fast.

Jacob makes the appropriate moaning sounds and throws down the sticks

A good throw! (*She looks at the sticks as they lie on the ground*) Well I never! A crooked crown!

Jacob What does that mean?

Anna Royalty is coming to my inn.

Jacob (*laughing*) Oh yes! His Majesty King Wenceslas is going to ride down from his golden statue!

They all laugh. Anna moves to the fireplace and pokes the fire

Anna Well, listen here: if the King, or the Chancellor for that matter, were to walk in here tonight, I'd tell them!

Jacob (*in disbelief*) Oh yes?

Anna I would, too! I'd say (*She grabs Jacob as if he were the King*) 'Look here King, or Chancellor, there are people starving while you eat your banquets.'

Jacob You never would!

Anna I'll drink to it! (*She raises her tankard*) Down with the King! Down with the Chancellor! Down with all taxes!

The King and the Page exchange glances and stand up, ready to leave. They put their tankards down on the table

King We must leave now, Mistress.

Anna Stay a while longer, sir. Have another drink. (*To Jacob*) Jacob, fetch the jug!

Jacob obeys

King Our journey this night has only just begun. (*He stretches his hand out to Anna; there are several gold coins in his open palm*) Take this, Mistress, and may better times come to Bohemia soon.

Anna (*looking in amazement at the coins*) But, sir, this is far too much ——

Jacob (*interrupting*) No, it's just right!

Anna makes to speak

(*Silencing Anna*) Farewell, pilgrims!

The King and the Page head for the exit

Anna Farewell — and good luck to you both!

King ⎱ (*on the point of leaving; together*) Farewell.
Page ⎰

The King and the Page exit

Anna We are going to have a Christmas after all! I'll be able to buy some presents for the children! (*To the Merchants*) You stay with us, travellers. We'll see you're all right!

Jacob. Come on, Anna. Let's have a song!

Anna and Jacob sing. As the song progresses the Merchants join in, both singing and dancing. The tune is the familiar one of 'Ten Green Bottles'

Song: Ten Fat Rats

Anna (*singing*)   Ten fat rats
Jacob   Sitting on the wall,
Merchants   Ten fat rats
                   Sitting on the wall
                   And if one fat rat
                   Should accidentally fall

They pretend to catch the falling rat in a saucepan

> There'd be nine fat rats
> Sitting on the wall.

The song continues in the traditional manner, getting faster and faster as it reaches the inevitable conclusion. When they reach the verse in which only two rats are left ...

The door opens and the Chancellor appears

Anna and Jacob both stop singing but the Merchants, in their innocence, continue until the bitter end. An awkward silence follows. Jacob looks at Anna to see if she will keep to her earlier threat. She starts sweeping the floor and continues to do so throughout the following dialogue

Jacob Good-evening, Chancellor. (*He fetches a drink for the Chancellor*)
Chancellor Cold night.
Jacob Very, Chancellor. Very cold.
Chancellor Business good, is it?
Anna Times are hard.
Chancellor I know, I know. Even for me. (*He pauses*). I wonder if you could help me? Have you seen a tall man — with a hood on — pass this way? (*To Anna*) I think the floor is clean enough now, Mistress. I repeat: have you seen a tall hooded young man pass by?
Anna As you were saying, Chancellor, the weather is very poor. Few travellers will venture out on a night as cold as this.
Chancellor (*looking at Jacob*) A tall man with a hood?
Jacob (*looking away*) No, no, Chancellor.
Chancellor That is a shame. I appear to have had a wasted journey. (*He moves over to the mantelpiece where he sees and picks up Anna's sugar mouse. He takes a knife from his pocket and cuts off the sugar mouse's head*)

The Merchants gasp

The Chancellor looks carefully at the Merchants

Anna Chancellor — my children's — Christmas ——

The Chancellor ignores her but goes on staring at the Merchants

Chancellor Not entirely wasted, perhaps. (*He sits close to the Merchants*) Strangers! And what brings you to Bohemia on this icy Feast of St Stephen?
Merchants The Christmas fair.
Chancellor The Christmas fair! Pedlars, are we? And have we paid our peddling tax?
First Merchant } (*together*) { Yes.
Second Merchant } { No.
First Merchant } (*together*) { No.
Second Merchant } { Yes.
Chancellor I thought not. That is very sad. For the penalties for non-payment of peddling tax are most, most severe. (*He stands and snatches the stick of holly from the mantelpiece. He brandishes it in front of the Merchants with his back to the fire*) They are the amongst the most severe penalties and punishments in the whole of Bohemia. Any idea what would happen to you?

There is a pause. The Merchants exchange very worried glances

Fortunately, things are not all bad. Here in Bohemia, if you do a favour for one person, that person may do a favour in return for you. If, for example, you were to tell a certain person that you had seen a tall person with a hood, it might be possible to overlook the payment. (*He eats the sugar mouse*) So — have we seen this tall person with a hood?

The Merchants nod

And this tall person with a hood — did he say where he was going?
First Merchant To St Agnes' fountain.
Chancellor Very good. Tell me now — was he alone or was there anybody with him?
Second Merchant A boy.
Chancellor I knew it! I knew it! (*He throws the holly onto the fire angrily. To the Merchants*) You've been most helpful. (*To Anna*) And it's a shame, Mistress, that your inn will have to close tomorrow.
Anna But we've paid our taxes!
Jacob It's not fair!

The Chancellor exits swiftly

A long pause. The Merchants look uneasily at each other

That's ruined our Christmas, that has.
First Merchant We are having to tell him. You hear what he is saying!
Anna (*angrily*) Now you hear what I am saying! Get out! We here in
   Bohemia don't tell tales on our brothers. Now, be off with you!
Jacob Traitors! Just like the sticks said!
Merchants But you cannot push us out!
Anna You heard the Chancellor — they're closing us down! Out!
Merchants But the weather — let us at least stay until morning!
Anna   Be off with you!

Anna ushers the protesting Merchants out of the door

(*Wearily collapsing in the chair*) Dear St Agnes — who can help us
now?

Music

SCENE 3

By St Agnes' Fountain

*The King and the Page, the latter still carrying the basket, struggle along
in a snowstorm during the following verse from the Storyteller. When they
reach the fountain, they find it is frozen. The Page collapses, unnoticed at
first by the King*

Storyteller   The news inside was harsh —
                        Less food and less fuel.
                        The wind outside was harsh,
                        Its icy breath like swords.

> But the King and the Page
> Struggled slowly on and on,
> Each footstep a new word
> Printed on the snow-blank sheet
> Of Bohemia's destiny.
>
> And when the two companions
> Reached St Agnes' fountain
> It was frozen in the earth
> Captive of the cruel Bohemian winter.

King At last! St Agnes' fountain! And the mountain towering above us like a great grey ghost. The old man's cottage must be close, Page! (*He notices the Page has collapsed*) Page! Come, we can't give up now. Not when we're nearly at the end of our journey!

Page Sire, I can't go a step further. My whole body is burning with cold, as if a fire of ice was consuming me.

King But to stay out here would mean certain death. Look! Over there — is that the poor man's cottage?

Page My eyes are weak but I believe it is, Sire.

King Then come. Let me help you up. (*He does so*) And I shall carry the basket now.

Page But Your Majesty — that would not be proper — it is a Page's duty to ——

King Kings have duties as well — to look after their subjects. No more words, Page. Lean on me and follow in my footsteps. We will soon reach the cottage.

Page (*aside*) No-one has ever spoken to me like that before — or helped me!

They move off slowly, the King singing the appropriate verse from the carol

King (*singing*) Mark my footsteps, good my Page,
                        Tread thou in them boldly.
                        Thou shall find the winter's rage
                        Freeze thy blood less coldly.

They exit slowly

Music

Narrator   Master and servant,
                     Servant and master,
                     Both help each other
                     Fight off the arrows of
                     Winter's white army.

                     While in the Poor Man's cottage,
                     Now in sight,
                     A father and daughter
                     Are fearful tonight.

SCENE 4

In the Poor Man's Cottage

The main room of a simple hovel with an empty fireplace and chimney of stone. A large high-backed settle is set to one side. A single candle is burning. The Poor Man and his young Daughter are on stage

Daughter But Father, I don't understand. Why did you go to the King's palace in the first place? You've always told me what a dangerous place it is!

Poor Man I had been searching everywhere for wood. The palace courtyard was the only place left in Prague with supplies of wood — and where they had cleared all the snow. I was desperate! I saw these spindly logs just lying in the corner and, well, I thought no-one would want them and no-one was looking. But as I bent down to pick up a log, why who should appear but the Chancellor himself!

Daughter They do say he has a thousand eyes! Oh Father!

Poor Man It's true. I had to run away — but I'm sure I saw someone following me through the snow.

Daughter If he catches you there's no telling what he'll do. Oh Father, you must hide. Quick, over in the corner with you.

The Poor Man goes to hide in the corner

Oh no, you can still be seen there. Behind the settle?

Poor Man Too obvious. That's the first place he'll look.
Daughter Oh dear!
Poor Man I'd rather be dead than see you come to any harm, Sara.
Daughter (*as if struck by an idea*) Perhaps if — no, it's too dangerous.
Poor Man Tell me, child — what is it?
Daughter Well, Father, if you were to pretend to be dead, then maybe the
    Chancellor would leave us alone. But I don't want to tempt Fate.
Poor Man It might work, Sara. Oh you always were a clever one — your
    poor mother would have been proud of you, God rest her soul.
Daughter Lie down here, Father, in the middle of the floor.
Poor Man (*lying on the floor*) Like this?
Daughter Yes. But a little flatter.

The Poor Man adjusts his position

    Yes, that's it. Now, how can we make you look a little paler?
Poor Man Rub snow in my face!
Daughter But it would melt, Father. No, we need something like — I
    know! Flour!
Poor Man Flour! But that's expensive. And we've hardly got any left.
Daughter Father, would you rather be dead for real?
Poor Man   Fetch the flour jar. It's by the chimney.

*The Daughter fetches the jar and smears flour all over the Poor Man's
face*

Daughter There, pale as a ghost. Oh I hope this won't bring us bad luck.
Poor Man It will be worse luck if the Chancellor catches me. You'd better
    bring me the coins.
Daughter Which coins?
Poor Man The two coins to pay the Ferryman on my journey to the Other
    World. They're hidden up the chimney.

The Daughter fetches two coins from the chimney

    I've been saving them for my funeral.
Daughter (*bringing the coins over to him*) Where shall I put them, Father?
Poor Man On my eyelids. (*He closes his eyes*)

The Daughter carefully places the coins over the Poor Man's closed eyes

I hope this works.

There is a loud knocking on the door

Daughter Father! He's here. What shall I do?
Poor Man Cry! Loud as you can!
Daughter (*crying*) Like this, Father?
Poor Man Louder!

The door opens

The Daughter throws herself on her knees and wails loudly. She does not see who is entering

  King Wenceslas enters carrying the basket, which he puts down on the floor; he then helps the Page to enter

King Page — is this the same poor man whom I first saw in the Palace Courtyard?
Page I think so, Sire.
King Then, it seems we have come too late.
Page Yes, Sire.
Daughter Oh woe is me! This is a sad house. My poor father is dead. We have no money!
King What are you saying?
Daughter We have no money to pay for taxes, Chancellor. And my father's dead. He didn't mean to steal the wood. This is a sad house.
King But we have not come to harm you or to take money for taxes. We have come to bring you food.
Daughter I don't understand. Why would you bring us food, Chancellor?
Page But he's not the Chancellor.
Daughter He isn't?
King No. I am the King.
Poor Man (*sitting bolt upright in a state of shock*) The King?

The King and the Page are amazed

King It seems he is alive again!
Poor Man (*looking at the coins which have fallen off his eyelids*) It is the

King, Sara. Look at his picture on the coins!

Daughter You're right, father.

Poor Man }
Daughter } (*kneeling; together*) Oh Sire! Forgive us!

Page Why were you pretending to be dead?

Daughter Because of the Chancellor.

Poor Man He is after me.

Daughter Everybody is so scared of him. He takes all our money for taxes. Now he'll surely throw my father into jail and me on to the snowy streets.

King (*silencing them with an imperial wave*) Don't worry any more. It is time I dealt with the Chancellor once and for all. But first — Page, fetch the basket.

Page (*bringing the basket closer*) We have brought you meat, wine and wood for your fire.

The Poor Man and the Daughter excitedly look at the gifts. The Page goes to look out of the window

Poor Man Just look at this, Sara!

Daughter Food fit for a King, Father.

Poor Man And wine, too! Look, look!

They break into a spontaneous dance

Page Sssh! Sire, I can see the Chancellor approaching.

The King looks out of the window too. The Poor Man and Daughter begin panicking

King Don't be scared. I am glad the Chancellor is here.

Poor Man }
Daughter } (*together*) Glad?

King Yes. Because I am going to teach him a lesson. (*To the Poor Man*) Now you lie down, friend, and pretend to be dead again. (*To the Daughter*) You cry just like you did before.

Page What about me?

King Come and hide behind the settle. Then we'll settle the Chancellor!

The King hurries behind the settle with the Page. The Poor Man settles down with the coins replaced on his eyelids and the Daughter kneels down, crying loudly as before

The door opens slowly. The Chancellor's hands appear first, then his head and finally the rest of his body. He keeps his distance from the Daughter at first

Chancellor I say, young 'un. Have you seen a tall man with a hood and a runaway Page passing this way? (*He approaches the Daughter*) I said, have you seen a ——— (*He stops as he notices the Poor Man*) Ah! The thief! Right! Now then, wood-stealer, your time has come. Are you listening to me? I will drag you personally all the way back to the capital and then horrible things will be done ... (*He pauses as he finally notices the lack of response from the Poor Man*) What's the matter with him? (*He pauses again*) I said, what's the matter with him?
Daughter Dead, Chancellor. Suddenly.
Poor Man Good. Serves him right for stealing wood from people.
Daughter He didn't mean to steal. It's just that we had nothing.
Chancellor It makes no difference now, does it ? (*He pauses, thoughtfully*) Has he paid his Death Tax?
Daughter (*crying*) We've no money to pay anything at all.
Chancellor A likely story. (*He notices the chimney and goes to search there*). I know you paupers, usually keep your money up the chimney. (*He finds something unpleasant and pulls his hand back in disgust. Then he notices the coins on the Poor Man's eyelids. He moves towards the Poor Man and takes the coins*) Ah! They'll do for a start.
Daughter But you can't take the coins off a corpse. They're to pay the Ferryman. It's bad luck.
Chancellor Bad luck for you. This should just about cover the Death Tax.

The Daughter throws herself down and clings to the hem of the Chancellor's coat

(*To the Daughter*) Get off! (*He pulls his coat free*) You can move out of this cottage tomorrow and we'll move someone else in who can afford to pay. (*He spots the basket brought by the King and the Page*)
Daughter Oh, you mustn't touch that!
Chancellor Seem to have seen this somewhere before. Oh well, keep me going for the rest of the journey. (*He lifts up the basket*)
Daughter Oh please, Chancellor.
King (*standing up and moving forward*) Stop! Put that basket down!
Chancellor Who are you to tell me to put this basket down?
King I am the King. (*He removes his hood*)

The Poor Man sits up and cheers. The Chancellor darts a look at him in amazement and fury, so the Poor Man quickly lies down again

Your time has come, Chancellor. I have made a journey tonight without your knowing. And this journey has taught me many things. You have lied to me!

Chancellor (*after a long pause*) Only a little.

King A little?

Chancellor Just to save you from getting depressed about the state of things in Bohemia.

King You told me the people were happy — that they had enough to eat, enough to drink, enough to keep themselves warm. Now I know you were lying. I find that my subjects are unhappy, hungry, thirsty and cold. And all because of you, Chancellor.

Chancellor But you enjoyed coming to the banquets, Sire. You were happy to have a statue covered in gold.

King That is true. But I no longer want to have such a statue.

Chancellor Very well. Just tell me. Tell me the changes you want to have made and I will fix it for you, Sire. Just leave it all in my hands. Tell me what to do.

King First of all, you can give me your gold chain.

Chancellor But really, Sire ——

King Come along!

The Page, the Poor Man and his Daughter watch, openly enjoying themselves

You said you would arrange any changes I wanted, Chancellor. Come along — give me the chain!

Chancellor But it's my Chain of Office!

King Correct! I no longer wish you to be my Chancellor.

The Chancellor reluctantly removes the chain from around his neck, watched by the delighted company. He makes to hand it to the King

No, on second thoughts — give it to these poor people. They need it more than I do.

Chancellor Oh really, Sire! They don't know what to do with money once they've got it. They just lie down and put it on their eyes!

King Give them the chain, Chancellor.

Slowly the Chancellor drops his chain into the waiting hands of the Poor Man and his Daughter

Now you must go. Out into the snow, the cold wilderness that is Bohemia. You must stay there for one year and a day. If you have learnt your lesson after that, then return and perhaps you may be Chancellor again.

The Chancellor moves towards the door

Poor Man Just before you go, Chancellor — well — the coins, please. For the Ferryman!

The Chancellor throws the coins onto the floor and the Poor Man picks them up. Then the Chancellor goes to the door, turns and calls out

Chancellor Page! Here!
Page (*moving after the Chancellor; then stopping*) No, I am staying with the King.

The Chancellor storms out and slams the door

King (*to the Page*) You may be my Page from now on — and juggle all you please. (*To the Poor Man and his Daughter*). Come, friends, and open the basket. Put logs on the fire. Let's celebrate.
Daughter May I invite our friends in?
King Of course. The more the merrier!

There is a flurry of activity as the Poor Man prepares the fire, the Page takes some cups out of the basket, the King pours drinks and the Daughter calls to her friends through the window

Daughter Come quickly. The King's here — and he's chased off the rotten old Chancellor and there's food and wine for everyone!
King Come now, let's sing a song together !

They form a line; the King stands in the middle

Poor Man What a good King Wenceslas!

*A group of Neighbours enters and they all sing the first three verses of
the carol*

All   Good King Wenceslas looked out
                           On the Feast of Stephen,
                           When the snow lay round about,
                           Deep and crisp and even.
                           Brightly shone the moon that night,
                           Though the frost was cruel,
                           When a poor man came in sight
                           Gathering winter fuel.

                           'Hither, page, and stand by me,
                           If thou knowst it telling,
                           Yonder peasant, who is he,
                           Where and what his dwelling?'
                           'Sire, he lives a good league hence,
                           Underneath the mountain,
                           Right against the forest edge
                           By St Agnes' fountain.'

                           'Bring me flesh and bring me wine,
                           Bring me pine-logs hither,
                           Thou and I will see him dine
                           When we bear them thither.'
                           Page and monarch, forth they went,
                           Forth they went together;
                           Through the rude wind's wild lament
                           And the bitter weather.

The Narrator steps forward

Narrator   And so our play draws to a close
                           With the Chancellor sent off
                           Into winter snows.
                           The poor are blessed
                           By a saintly King

Whose name each Christmas time
We stand and sing.
We thank you for listening,
Our kind friends,
But now we are finished
Our story ends.

CURTAIN

FURNITURE AND PROPERTY LIST

ACT I

SCENE 1

On stage: Gold chain of office
              Crown
              Log
              Joint of meat on platter
              Jug of wine
              Page's cap
              Juggling balls

SCENE 2

On stage: Table. *On it*: plates of meat, poultry, fish, cakes
              Large chair
              Goblets of wine for **King** and **Chancellor**
              Jug of wine for **Third Servant**
              Basket of logs for **First Servant**
              Tray of food for **Second Servant**

Personal: **Narrator**: puppet

SCENE 3

On stage: Pile of logs

Off stage: Lance (**Chancellor**)

SCENE 4

On stage: Chest. *In it*: hood
              Jug of wine
              Goblet for **King**

ACT II

SCENE 1

Off stage: Basket containing meat, wine, logs, cups (**Page**)

SCENE 2

On stage: Rocking chair
            Two benches
            Table. *On it*: jug, tankards
            On mantelpiece: meagre Christmas decorations, including a
                stick of holly, a sprig of pine, a red ribbon and a sugar mouse
            Tankards for **Merchants**
            Saucepan
            Broom

Off stage: Basket (as SCENE 1) (**Page**)
            Bag containing carpets and clothes, including a Persian rug
                and a brocade waistcoat (**First Merchant**)
            Bag containing puppet (**Second Merchant**)

Personal: **King**: Velvet purse containing gold coins
            Chancellor: Knife

SCENE 3

Off stage: Basket (as SCENE 1) (**Page**)

SCENE 4

On stage: Settle
            Candle
            Jar of flour
            Two coins

Off stage: Basket (as SCENE 1) (**Page**)

LIGHTING PLOT

Various interior and exterior settings
Practical fittings required: log fire

ACT I

To open:　General lighting

Cue 1　　**Narrator: 'Come!'**　　　　　　　　　　(Page 5)
*Cross-fade to Banqueting Hall lighting
with fireglow effect on fire*

Cue 2　　**Narrator: 'In the story he had heard.'**　　(Page 12)
Cross-fade to Palace Courtyard lighting

Cue 3　　**The Servants exit**　　　　　　　　　　(Page 16)
*Cross-fade to Private Chamber lighting
with fireglow effect on fire*

ACT II

To open:　General exterior lighting

Cue 4　　**The Chancellor exits. Music**　　　　　(Page 24)
*Cross-fade to Inn lighting with fireglow effect
on fire*

Cue 5　　**Anna: '...who can help us now?'**　　　(Page 35)
Cross-fade to general exterior lighting

Cue 6　　**Narrator: 'Are fearful tonight.'**　　　(Page 37)
*Cross-fade to cottage lighting with covering
spot on candle*

EFFECTS PLOT

ACT I

No cues

ACT II

Cue 1   As Scene 3 begins   (Page 35)
            Snowstorm effect

9 780573 165016